4/13

Genius Loci

Genius Loci

Poems by

Lance Larsen

UNIVERSITY OF TAMPA PRESS

Manufactured in the United States of America
Printed on acid-free paper ∞
First Edition

On the Cover: "Humming Chair" by Jacqui Larsen

The University of Tampa Press
401 West Kennedy Boulevard
Tampa, FL 33606

ISBN 978-159732-103-7 (hbk.)
ISBN 978-159732-104-4 (pbk.)

Browse & order online at
http://utpress.ut.edu

Library of Congress Cataloging-in-Publication Data

Larsen, Lance, 1961-
 [Poems. Selections]
 Genius Loci : poems / by Lance Larsen. -- First edition.
     pages cm
 Includes bibliographical references and index.
 ISBN 978-1-59732-103-7 (hbk) -- ISBN 978-1-59732-104-4 (pbk)
 I. Title.
 PS3562.A738G46 2013
 811'.54--dc23   2012045116

Contents

For Jacqui, once again

"—Nothing happens? Or has everything
happened, and we are standing now,
quietly, in the new life?"

—Juan Ramón Jiménez

"The air is full of secrets.
Just by breathing,
you become my accomplice."

—Elaine Equi

I

Chancellor of Shadows

Horses are praying the old fashioned way, trotting
a fenced field at twilight under a towel of moon.

Swans settle on the pond, like a five-paragraph essay
on beauty. Yes, we have our rituals, like the skunk

stitching one pulsing patch of shadow to the next
with the swish of its tail. Not to mention questions.

How many broken pies at the bakery dream
the forgiveness of hungry mouths? How many

weeks till the silverfish chews through Chaucer?
What if the other life is buried inside this one?

A stack of bricks, a work shirt billowing on the line:
epics in the making. Each set of doubts, a path.

Like the owl, I'll take my wages in mice and falling
stars, take my midnights in the middle of the day.

Why Do You Keep Putting Animals
in Your Poems?

I open windows to catch a glimpse of *grace*
on the horizon, and in they sneak, coyotes and crows,
pikas and the scholarly vole, dragging scoured skies
I can see myself in. Much cheaper than booking
a flight to the Galápagos. And they teach me.

Badgers rarely invent stories to make them sad
about their bodies. And the wrinkliest of Shar Pei
never dreams of ironing its face. My happiness
is like a flock of sparrows that scatters when a bus
drives by, then re-strings itself two blocks away,

a necklace of chirps festooning a caved-in barn.
Lemurs will bite a millipede to release narcotic
toxins, then hand it to a neighbor as if passing
a joint at a concert. In a Rhode Island nursing home,
Oscar the miracle cat curls up with residents

hours before they expire, converting death into purrs
for the next world. A poem is grave and nursery:
the more creatures you bury in one place,
the more hunger bursts forth somewhere else,
like bats at Carlsbad when the brightest day turns dusk.

The night I stood on my sister's feet and learned
to waltz, a porcupine braved four lanes of asphalt
and hurtling machines to chomp our windfall apples—
two miracles of syncopation held together by a harvest
moon. As Marianne Moore taught us, an hour

at the Bronx Zoo in a tricorn hat leaves one happier
than nine months with a shrink. Comes a time
you have to wiggle your pinfeathers,
wag your ghost tail, feel your teeth grow long
for the ragged salmon throwing their bodies upstream.

A Bright Darkness
Sometimes Mistaken for Fishing

He flipped the trout, as if re-positioning a book
in his hands, then sliced from anus to sunset,
sunset to quivering chin, clean like the line
where water licked shore. We were trapped
in dusk, the two of us, my father thigh deep
in river, me in wet tennis shoes. He plunged
thumb and finger into the fish and pulled

till the insides peeled free. He held that slither
of organs at arm's length, as if hanging
wind chimes on a porch, then side-armed them
into the willows. Was it then or later
we traded bodies? Whatever we came for—
the water's blood pull, the blue vacancy of sky
one can hook but never reel in—beyond us now.

He creeled that trout, then rinsed his hands.
But still it clung—a fish-slippery something
that glazed the car door, printed the Coke
bottle we shared, coated the radio dial
that searched the chaos for a voice to warble
us home. We drove east, the river held west,
and I had all evening to swap places with the dark.

Catch eleven fish, fail. Catch none, again fail.
When he tousled my hair, I leaned in
to feel night up close. I was a swirl
of buggy water, my father the breeze, the sky
dreamed in scales, my happiness closed
and opened like gills, the ones we're born with
and spend our best breath forgetting how to use.

Nothing Happy

Nothing happy with what it is—not evening, not noon,
not the stolid pear trying to blush like a peach,

not the soprano who leases her voice to jealous stars.
An elevator waits to be translated into a school bus,

Memorial Day pines to dress up as Halloween.
Make us into gardens, we pray, let our fists grow

feathers, let the earth swallow our mistakes like ash.
So much impatience, pencils wishing they were forks, trees

dreaming of combing the sky. If only the bored broom
could sweep up a grave, if only the dice in the alley

could learn to roll like teeth. We are each a bingo parlor
dreaming of a knife fight, a worn copy of *Ulysses* hoping

to be burned. Another swerving car, another splayed
deer on the county road waiting to be tutored by rain.

Blood says, I've always wanted to travel by myself.
Spirit whispers, finally a chance to grow my own fur.

Garden of Earthly Delights

Never mind that we could barely make rent,
never mind that the lady in 3-A
sold lingerie door to door, and her hubbie
practiced taxidermy on armadillos
in their kitchen. We knew our souls
were worth nurturing because junked cars
kept igniting across the street,
and cicadas dismantled everything green.

Then the mail carrier mispronounced
our new checks by three buildings,
and two Egyptian brothers,
Omar Thin and Omar Stout, bounced
our surnames and misspelled our desire
all over the city. Still we made friends.
Here's to the squirrel that climbed
the telephone pole to beg marmalade toast.

Here's to the broken-backed piñata hanging
by its birthdays from the locust tree,
and to the police helicopter
that mistook you for someone
with initiative, and me for someone
carrying a filched VCR, and fixed
us both in stabs of white light.
Along came Labor Day, and our neighbor

asking us to store her piano in our bedroom
while she helped her diabetic aunt
in Waco exit this world
one amputated toe at a time.
We said yes and the weather still darkened.
Because it was a holiday, partiers
tossed their empties into the deep end,
and a pair of chocolate Labradors paddled

figure eights. Because the pending
hurricane filibustered all evening,
then ended in blackout, we stayed in.
The flickering of three candles
reminded us an open book
sometimes equals a country,
and a bedroom floats like an ark.
Brahms had been hiding in your fingers

so long that when you released him,
we fell into animal elegance and listened
with our hair, asked questions
with our breath. We feared sleep.
Knew how morning would pin
us to our names again—
the old ones we spent half the dark
and most of each other trying to rub off.

Elegy, with City Bus and Blue-haired Girl

If three things made her beautiful waiting
                    to board the 822,
          five left her lost, though in a month of Thursdays

I could never name them. From my seat,
                    I could tally
          colors—hair several shades of darkening

sky, a shopping list in green scribbled
                    up and down
          her left arm. Or was it a manifesto?

She was the last in line, so I had plenty
                    of time not
          to fall in love. Bright but cold outside,

one of those March mornings when if
                    you're a body
          of water, it's better to flow shallow

than run deep—more surface to suck up
                    a feeble sun.
          But also more brooding, more vulnerability,

more time for a boy with a shaved head to cut
                    in front of her
          before she stepped on. They faced

each other, his back to the bus door.
                    Not this time
          he said without saying, and crossed

his arms in leather. Such things happen
            in Newark
        or outside boarded-up Conoco stations

dreaming of recreational arson, but not here:
            not in the shadow
        of Lincoln Middle School—where custodians

emptied garbage in French, and ivy falling across
            the teacher's desk
        taught everyone to photosynthesize, breathe in,

one two three, even on chilly days, even if a girl
            with blue hair
        kept saying, *Don't bring it, don't bring it, don't bring it.*

But he had brought it, his body a gate
            that wouldn't swing,
        a locked gate that turned everything public.

Lost Girl vs. Loser Boy. A hush hung
            between them,
        against which she tried to move. He countered.

Lovers these two, you could tell, by the way
            they touched
        with their eyes. They had entered burning

buildings in tandem, counted petals
            and uncles
        on parole, tic-tac-toed the constellations

from a broken mattress under a bridge—
            only not now.
                Now she shoulder-butted him, and he pushed

back. Which made three of us stand up,
                and two of us
                    reach for our cells. But *no,* not a push exactly,

something short of that, a meanness you could
                get away with
                    at bus stops, under the trembling of a red-tailed

balloon caught in overhead branches
                that should
                    have signaled desire, but just hung there, a rag.

And the school bell, when it sounded, rang
                out advice: *Save her,*
            push him away, try anything. But if we tried,

he'd just give it to her worse later on,
                wouldn't he?
                    Whatever *It* was. *It* pushed down on us,

tasted the air we drew into our mouths,
                dripped from the bus
                    to pool at their ankles. Then children poured

out for recess. "Miss, do you need some help?
                Hey, Miss."
                    The driver punctuated his offer with tenderness:

he knelt the bus. Yes, knelt it. In a whoosh
                of hydraulics,
            that behemoth dinosaured to its knees.

Which offered her something—seconds
                and second chances,
            offered her a pause, chivalric and ridiculous,

in which children dodge-balled and four-squared,
                and all of us
            dropped fifteen inches out of our newspapers

and complacence. Offered. Plenty of time
                for her to say *yes*.
            She shifted, looked away, then broke into a run,

back the way she had come, toward the river.
                Mr. Leather
            followed her, taking his time to flash

the bus a scowl and scrape his boots across
                the grass,
            as if wiping us off forever. Then the bus rose.

Americana

I found her yard strewn with garbage—a confetti
of junk mail and potato peels, trash can
knocked over—and Old Lady Kuhni herself
in a purple kimono thing trying to clean up.
"Wild dogs done this," she said, followed by complaints
about her Jack, "damn him, he gone up
the mountain to shoot him another deer, and could you,
please . . ." Who was I to turn her down?
I was a paper boy on foot, thrower of bad news.

So I stooped and gathered—charred toast,
wallets of dryer lint, bloodied wads of t.p.,
grapefruit rinds like speckled snakes.
When she handed me a badminton racquet,
I thought, "A gift?—why not, I've earned it."
Then she motioned me to the fence
and pointed. Lying in a bed of scraggly mums,
a deer head. Prim as a handbag, but chewed,
one eye missing, the other staring across frosted lawn.

She knew boys like me were brave in stupid ways
and wouldn't mind using a racquet
as a spatula. So I scooped up
that face and carried its soft ears and final
grimace across the yard. Carried it.
We're always auditioning for something.
Old Lady Kuhni: a little respect.
That partitioned deer: a blind date with eternity.
Me: for paper boy of the decade, plus tips.

Which is why I carried its face like a torch.
"Not in the trash," she said, "that would bring
the dogs again." I followed her into the garage
instead, to the freezer, which gasped
in white, a cauldron filled with dry ice.
I settled that face atop a bed of frozen peas,
and she closed the lid. We traded then.
I handed her the racquet, handle first,
and she buried me in thank-yous. Then I trudged

back into that cold masquerading as Sunday
morning. What I didn't know
hung everywhere. Tricky Dick Nixon
and the price of bananas from my shoulders,
secret lives from lit windows.
I was a carrier, worth 87 cents a day,
plus rubber bands, right arm two inches
longer than my left. I looked back
then and saw in the side yard the rest of the doe—

upside down, in an apple tree, tied in place
with a blue jump rope,
rib cage stuck open with kindling.
What I breathed out was only breath
but felt like moths.
Moths that climbed and dissolved,
climbed and dissolved, till I too circled
that exquisite scarecrow of hanging
meat, weddings and want ads banging my thighs.

Tired

I'm tired of the usual—foofy dogs, West End
musicals, Edgar Allan Poe.
Also leather jackets and the posers
who wear them, believing a carcass
across the back brings Hell's Angels cool.

I'm especially tired of not having one myself.
Tired of tragedy ending
badly, gullible Hamlet taking the word
of a rasping ghost.
Tired of talk about the tinctured light

of Provence and the sacred tintinnabulations
of Florentine shadows,
especially my own yak yak yak,
as if I now grasped Renaissance metaphysics
thanks to frequent flyer miles.

I'm tired of the word *tired*.
Shouldn't it drag along, multiple-syllabled,
like *remonstration* or *jeremiad,* drag
with eleven vowels packed
together and a Maori death sentence hanging

over my head if I fail to pronounce each one?
Tired too of diagrams explaining
the collapse of the twin towers,
but no mention of the kaleidoscopic flight
of ghosts. And of course I'm tired of Time.

Big hand saying, Mr. Death, Kahuna
of all Kahunas, he be waiting
for you up ahead. Little hand saying, Never,
never in this life. Meanwhile some invisible
sundial turning in my chest,

like the Spanish Inquisition, counting lost
seconds and saying, This heart,
baby, it's all you got. Tired of remembering
my brat of a niece texting
one of her dipstick friends the night my father died.

Texting beside his rest home bed,
when she should have memorized
the stale air, bruises on his arm linked
like the Great Lakes,
the orange pad on the floor in case he rolled off,

the way he twisted and bucked in his sleep,
picking up one leg,
then the other, as if climbing
a mountain straight into the sky,
not knowing which foot to put down next.

II

Backyard Georgics

Gone the homeland, gone the father,
       nothing left but invisible north
   to magnetize your doubts.

*

     One clock for errands,
one for midnight trysts,
   though neither will hurry a slow train.

*

A lightning strike to test
      the *gestalt* of stillness, an apron
   of lambent stars to taste the dark.

*

     Interview or early wake?
A birdbath at noon in which
   you glimpse your own plashy face.

*

Is a snake touched thrice one snake
      or three? What is the opposite
   of *rapture of the deep?*

*

Prairie is not the floor nor sky
the coffered ceiling. Even a scarecrow
is wise beyond its straw.

*

Teach me to clench deep,
          like the honey locust in fall,
     then shake shake shake my terrible thorns.

*

Orchard gone feral, sky dark
as Ecclesiastes: when I sliced
     the peach, tiny moths flew out.

*

It takes a calendar one damp day
          to declare fall, weeks of dying
     mums to second the motion.

*

First frost: a trio of robins
at the dryer vent bathing
     in the lacy breeze of tumbling bras.

*

Look down: a river of grass. Look up:
          a velvet lost and found. Look inside:
     no straws to drink that dusk.

*

      Not eulogies or hearses
but the sandwiches after, estranged
     cousins chewing under one umbrella.

*

Little Dipper whispering *sip,*
         but which unholy spring will leave us
     whole, which gods dare we drink?

*

      Woman's watch thieved by a jay—
ah, to be lifted like that, carried
     like time across lapping waves.

Rough Translation

I slip outside into a corridor of clarity and breeze—
that pinking time when owls home to barns, when bats

fold their genius into gloves of sleep and cranes
whoop in the morning like freckled boys on stilts.

One body: some days, I swear, one is almost enough.
But not today. Today let me dissolve in narcotic dark,

squeeze into this broken parable we call first light.
Grief and wind, meadow and awe. Who will teach

me to listen with leaves, make sky my skin? I lean,
wondering which of my faces morning will erase first.

A Magpie's Hop

Call us a hard, scrabbled people who trust
seared air more than grace. How could we

pretend otherwise in our fretted world of dust?
We live by axioms of the gut: we witch

for water, tender treaties with the sun, build
crooked houses that mimic crooked skies.

Who can explain a beauty so cleanly thin?
A blouse of lichen takes centuries to sew.

A magpie's hop measures the horizon's pull
better than surveyors. Wind jabbers amen.

When will the desert blossom like a rose?
The locust is our tormentor, the hummingbird

sipping nectar at dusk our longshot truth.
Patience is an argument water always wins.

Man in a Suit,
Twelve Crickets in His Pocket

I'm a man who hates to make an extra trip,
who buys a dozen feeder crickets
on his way to the wedding reception.

Back home, my son's tarantula waits,
caged in its glassy cravings, cleaning its fangs.
Everything must eat: crickets eat

my son's allowance, my headlights eat
the asphalt of an icy road, in a parked car
the cold will finish crickets in nine minutes.

Therefore I enter the reception with twelve
hopping warriors stuffed in my coat pocket.
Gifts eat the table and dribble their lush

ribbons to the floor, signatures eat the snowy
blankness of the guest register. If I swing
my coat, the crickets forget to chirp.

Think of me as a man distressed by January,
a man who holds a newly minted couple
at the end of his right arm—bodies lit

and burning. His and hers, shake.
Matching teeth and "I do's," shake.
Getaway car soaped with innuendo, shake.

I'm a man with seven holes in his head,
a man jiggling his pocket who takes his slice
of wedding cake into the night—breathe

in cold, breathe out light, fire up my car.
And now I'm a man holding still at red lights,
willing dark voices to sing away the dark.

Till death do us part, chirr. Legs, eyes,
antennae, chirr. Hopping at my hip, chirr.
Now it begins: that crickety song that trawls

the emerald lawns of June for a boy
sleeping out, for a man in winter listening
for his name and the electric hush that follows.

Tabernacle

How many minutes does it take a gut-shot
buck to helter-skelter through skree
and lose the hunter? How many days
for turkey vultures to convert death
into gliding? How many years

till some schlub hiker like me stumbles
upon the remains? There it lay—
a tableau in bleached bone, flight
and collapse converted into sleep.
Hooves and vertebrae, laddered ribs:

I touched till I felt time chewing me
from the inside, as it must have chewed
this deer. I lay down and woke an hour
later to smoke—fire across the lake,
the afternoon turned apocalyptic by haze.

I plucked sage, flicked an ant from my shoe,
swallowed ashy air, glassed the slow
syntax of scrub oak giving way
to power lines and cul-de-sacs till I found
my house, relic of some former life.

I rose to my feet then, placed my boot
on that scoured skull and wrenched.
One antler cracked free, then the next.
Picking my way down, I felt
like a messenger who knows not

what thrumming truth he has tasted,
what questions hang from his antlered
hands. Wavery with sun, my house
looked like an ark floating away
before I could bow my head and climb on.

Owning the Snake

Gorgeous and unnerving, the way he laddered
           his body, all six feet of him, up to the first branch,
      then used the collateral of his own sinewy loops

to cantilever himself higher, limb by limb,
           rising in the pear tree like some highly evolved law
      of deceit: awe zeroing my blood, sun dropping,

my daughter beside me tensing at trespass.
           Hadn't I nursed this oasis out of dust and thorn?
      Therefore, the evening. Therefore, everything in it.

Then we heard chirpings, and thus tasted
           ruin—five robin mouths aimed at the sky,
      and an assassin in the tree. I bolted for a hoe.

When I returned, the snake had gulped
           a pair of nestlings, my daughter waist deep
      in her own cries. I reached till I hooked a loop

of the intruder, who hissed his ire at me.
           Call him Blow Snake, Hogback, Puff Adder.
      I pulled. He caught and draped, caught again,

like an old feud wedged in the bones
           of enmity. But names fail and bodies fall.
      Once he hit the battered ground

he hissed in earnest, filled with escape.
           Smash him, my daughter yelled, *smash him*.
      I held. He limped off through unmown grass,

if a snake can limp, like a fallen prophet
　　　　　　　trying to part the waters. Two lives lost,
　　　but three saved. Or four, if you count the snake,

all flash and flesh, all swimming glide,
　　　　　　　this serpent I thought I owned, taking
　　　some swallowed part of us into a darker fold.

The Most Spider Part of Me

1

On the fifth morning I woke to a palace of silk—a spider web stretched across my open closet. My fortune for clapping up a cat face in a jar but neglecting to tighten the lid.

2

Gossamer guarding my shirts: more true than magnetic north. Like having an unfolded map to the underworld as a bedside lamp.

3

Each morning I misted the web. The slightest breeze caused those tendrils to fling light around the room, like a shield at the mouth of a cave.

4

Each time I tossed a moth into that labyrinth, I turned accomplice—and interpreter of spider idioms. Daintying out of hiding with her lethal speed: *Thank you, but I prefer to work alone.* Administering her bite: *What did you expect, the foxtrot?* Entombing her victim in silk and setting it swinging: *Prudence is as prudence does.*

5

Let each of her legs stand for a lost garden, each cat face stripe hang fear on the air. Let her eyes search out my secrets but share them with no one.

6

Of course I apologized each time I broke her web reaching for socks. Like praying to a god who lives on a ledge above my life. But how, how do I say amen?

7

O mercurial! O copacetic! O chiaroscuro! Words I fell in love with later, but which always take me back to filaments and sun, legs like syllables, yearning that fills the body.

8

Not so much death in the room where I slept, but ritual and art, and a dark hum that was both and neither. Was I the fanged spider, spinnerets wetly glowing? Or the moth, paid down like a parachutist tangled in power lines?

9

Soon the foothills would give up and sign a lease with winter. Soon the moon would fatten with desire. Soon my parents would put down their paperbacks and repeat the glorious error that brought me into the world.

10

Or was I the web itself—nerved grid, sacrificial hammock?

11

Years later, I would think of that latticework as wisdom. This is how love ends, how poems begin, here waits faith with its sharpened fangs, here lies my latest bible of doubt. Call that filigree the Esperanto we speak in dreams: teach me to spool out of my body, make holy this seance of thirsts.

12

Can you hear that siren song still purling from the wings?

13

Three days after Thanksgiving I found her on the floor—yellowed pearl, elegy with curled legs. No will and testament written into the web, no anguish brigade. I rolled her gently between finger and thumb, like a pill one swallows to recall past lives, then buried her in snow.

III

Make of Me

Dirt combed free of tracks twice a day,
tree trunks whitewashed as high

as arthritis can reach. Make of me,
late fall, what this bent peasant has made

of her poverty. Flung potato water
gleaming on bricks outside her window,

an albino dog licking up what is wet
if not holy, legs splayed to keep paws dry.

Adding a Ghost-like Hum to Your Inner Life

A sleeping tabby is the easiest way to add
stripes to a living room. Scylla
and Charybdis, Heloise and Abelard,
the gusting breeze and the meter reader's
fabulous red hair: choose only one duet.
My son asks, "Would you rather be
the president's bodyguard or a rare
Chinese custard eaten by your one true love?"

Unless you've attended medical school,
never massage the brain directly.
Fine, lie down naked as Adam, as long
as you rise up wise as Eve. Cultivate paradox,
like the brooding diarist who doubts
the world *until* she writes it down, then doubts
the world *because* she writes it down.
If supernal beauty will not hold still, chill

in the fridge for twenty minutes, then snap
its picture. (More effective for a praying mantis
than northern lights.) Neglect not Archimedes
or interviews with a mirror that doubles
as a pond of feeding fish. Neglect not
serendipitous gifts, as when a crying
child finds a broken globe at the dump
and leaves wearing Tierra del Fuego as a helmet.

In this waiting room called Planet Earth,
we are all stenographers of the sublime.
Cistercian monks knew that if you
ring two bells a whole step apart,
your ear will catch a distant third tone
that isn't there. If an ant crosses
your kitchen table, give her a name,
then carry her into the sun on a dirty fork.

What Bliss, When Exuberance Overruns Its Banks

As in a certain exit ramp outside Seattle,
a glissando of cement and steel
that promised release, or at least a shortcut
to the Sound, then sheered off into sky.

As in stretches of Hemingway when dialogue tags
fall off the page, leaving only God
and a passing scrap of cumulus   .
to discuss troutness vs. the ontology of clean.

As in my favorite Rembrandt etching:
milkmaid canoodling with her beau, spokes
of sun above, hay at her back, why
the hell shouldn't she reach with three arms?

After De Chirico

In the subway station, a man wearing my face
lies across the tracks.
Each time he tries to rise electricity
surges through him, so he rests,
still as a medieval city
the Renaissance has passed by.
I hurry to his side, but never draw any closer.

Commuters tall as trees stare with camera
faces. Pigeons weave
a perfect figure eight above him.
Finally, the gardener arrives, damp gloves
still on, and covers the man
with a giant blue wing, to keep
him warm, to hide the approaching train.

Between the Heaves of Storm

We have buried our aunt with words
and hymns. Now to finish the job with dirt.
In the front of the church, a hearse waits
to lead the cortège of headlights to the cemetery.
But here, in the back parking lot,
a grandniece, perhaps six, has squirmed
out of her itchy skirt and grabbed

a pink hula hoop from the family van.
We put the morning on pause,
three or four of us, car doors flung open.
Plenty of time to take in this emptying quiet,
her skirt puddled now on asphalt
like a staircase into the underworld.
And plenty of room for her little girl hips.

She jounces and gyrates, as if trying
to coax rain out of the wispy clouds
floating above our fair city.
Twelve, thirteen, fourteen . . . She counts
with a wheezy underwater voice,
the kind one uses to address homemade dolls—
limp dolls, badly stitched, x's for eyes,

velcro on the hands to hold an embrace
after the arms grow tired.
Little grandniece swings her hips.
Green undies, dishrag sky, a waiting
that fills the parking lot even as it clears.
Any worries about the next life set spinning
for now in reassuring orbits, rattly pink.

When the Lord Returns
in His Creaturely Perfection

He will burrow and gallop, buffalo the prairie
again, penguin the unhatched egg,
then sleep off centuries of miracles
with the three-toed sloth. What a magician,
one minute pirouetting among banks
of altostratus, the next grazing
underground cafés with the star-nosed mole.

Out of caves, from under bridges, a million
translations of a single verb,
limp body lifted in the vulture's beak.
Surely this time, Lord, we will know
the declensions of your ministry.
One day a rat, the next hundred
years a raccoon, both doing pastoral care

among the wino savants of south Chicago.
Now you twig back and forth,
a Madagascar walking stick,
now you manatee the mangroves.
Does your thirst fill one camel hump
or two? Carry our griefs two nautical
miles below the song of plunging narwhales.

Soon you will fill the globe and we will taste
your bounty, in every shadow,
every flicker of indigo sky, like a flock
of doves passing overhead,
wide as Nebraska, inexhaustible,
something perverse daring us to shoot
you out of that faithful air, and we probably will.

IV

To the Ode

True, you intimidate me, but when I slip you on,
like Horace's bathrobe, all things spark

to life: an ant as worthy of praise as a phoenix,
plastic cup as capacious as Grecian urn.

Nothing too trivial for you—not clouds, not the bent
spoon carrying gruel to the dowager's mouth,

not spotted dogs in heat. Thanks to you, I talk
to my orange juice before I drink it, I begin

a Q and A with the rain, greed converted into awe,
an ancient Mayan city behind my sternum.

What is water, but a confessor, happy to wash away
my grit? What are train tracks but a ladder

to heaven turned on its side? What is a rotting
mouse but a country of flies buzzing with praise?

To Alchemy

Salt crystals turning into sea monkeys, salamanders
into witches, a sip of wine into the jeweled blood
of God. I've always loved your presto change-o
miracles. Here I am, middle-aged
and mortgaged, and still I believe.
Sitting down to play Chopin, I hope
to be converted into electric mist
or a flock of wrens. When my father died,
I went bowling—anything to transform
the avalanche behind my breastbone
into crashes I could hear. After my third game,
I tossed down fifty dollars and walked
away wearing grief size twelve and a half,
grief in shades of smoke and blood
I could lace myself. We need you, Alchemy,
because darkness beckons, because the body
bruises easily, can't fly or burrow,
can never find the ignition in the time machine.
Some evenings all I want to do is dial
the dead, or redecorate my garden
using fallen stars and the cat in my lap.
Just once let me take a bath
in fire, then hatch anew from my ashes.
Just once let me be a sophomore again.
Make it the Friday before Christmas,
me beside the Coke machine
in the school gym holding mistletoe
above my head: waiting for nirvana to walk by
in a drill team sweater and ghostly
perfume, and convert my blind mouth into a kiss.

To Duende

I've traced the face of a deer seven minutes dead,
cut the umbilical of my glistening son.
You blessed me in those days, why not now?
You are the bones of my waiting, the blood
of my hurry, the breath inside my breath.

Wasn't it Lorca who said you do not haunt
the throat so much as climb from the soles
of the feet? When will you climb through me?
You bless flamenco and bullfights, never
croquet. I will try more broken glass, more dark

knowing: teach me to scratch my doubts
on cave walls and subway cars. Which totemic
craving should I steer by today? I will hide
behind banter and brie, weekend tête-à-tête
but inside—magpie, weasel, skunk, snake . . .

Fire in the pocket, windstorm in the skull, you.
The way a groan searches for a mouth,
or a scream fills a pair of lungs, you. I will cut
off the wings of my daytime angel, eat earth
three days straight, drink rain from my dirty fur.

To Jouissance

To spell you is to drown in vowels, to pronounce
you is to let guttural *joy* form in the back
of my throat, then roll forth,
like northern lights booming above a logging
camp in Michigan. Disappointed
in my metaphor? What did you expect from a man?

If only I had an estrogen factory of my own.
If only I could feel the fluttery,
everywhere *she*-pleasure you bring to lucky
women. I mean the buzz that overtakes
a new mother nursing in a booth at Denny's,
eyes blissing out, body serenely electric.

I mean whatever state my cousin Erica falls
into when someone braids her hair
in the middle of church—simple Erica
who washes tables at McDonald's
but can't read a menu. She knows
enough to close her eyes and give pleasure

more room, knows enough to let purrs
bubble from her mouth, the liquid gold
on her head dividing into glorious threes,
my jealousy tripling. Do you sometimes
make exceptions and visit not just
the Ericas of the world, but the Erics?

I'm thinking of the twenty-something kid
last week who popped up from his seat
and ran to the front of the bus.
That's my old man, he said, pointing
to the cement truck stopped beside us
at a red light. *Hey Dad, I'm over here, look*,

and Ernie, our glum undertaker of a driver,
broke the rules for once and swung
open the door at an intersection.
Surely you must have blessed that transaction:
grizzled duffer and tattooed boy leaning
towards each other, like a pair of gargoyles,

air crackling between them. The light turned
green, the afternoon sped up, and the duffer
said, *Hey Tommy, nice hat, you ready
for bowling Saturday night?—take her easy.*
Who can explain where the world ends and a son
begins, how molecules of longing map the flesh?

They waved, father and son, like they'd never
see each other again in this time zone.
And we watched: starved, eavesdropping citizens
of the bus, remembering some ecstasy
we fell into once and didn't deserve, sitting
on our hands to keep from adding amens to the air.

To My Insomnia

Perhaps if I had sung more Christmas hymns
as a child or gone to summer camp
in the Adirondacks, I wouldn't suffer you now.
Perhaps if I had read more *Newsweek,*
less Nietzsche. I wander like Lady Macbeth,
washing my bloody hands in moonlight,
then rearranging the spoon drawer.
Where will your foreplay lead tonight—

to another dark night of the soul
or Jackie Chan reruns? In my twenties
you ignored me. Now, every few days, you ease
under my front door, a miasmal ooze.
Haven't all the great thinkers suffered you?
But also most addicts of the Shopping Channel.
I have wrestled ontologies in you,
then wandered the neighborhood, a loiterer,

a malingerer in dirty socks, a stalker hoping
to be taken in by a forgiving ex.
Some have a good shrink in the Avenues,
or a sympathetic priest. I have you.
Or rather you have me. Or rather we both
have the ascetic hum of the fridge
at 3:00 a.m., which invites me to caterwaul,
to bow to the lesser gods of the deep freeze.

You have taught me how to swill stars
and flirt with ghosts, how to perform exegesis
on dim all-night diners, meringues leaning
like bedraggled widows. I fear and loathe you,
true, but a week without your midnight
innuendo and I feel spurned like that girl
in Honors English everyone cheats
off of by day, but never invites to the drive-in.

To My Muse

When I ask for step-by-step instructions,
you tell me to eavesdrop on blue
herons, to wash in dust,
to take dictation from urban rain.
When I ask where you live,
you say, *Can floating spores be parsed?*

When I attempt to nap my humble way
toward the sublime, you toss
a talking pig into my dreams.
When I shout, "Huzzah!"
you caution that testosterone
is a dangerous fuel to think with.

When I try to footnote desire, you say,
*Who can extract sunlight
from a field woozy with pollen and mating
dragonflies?* When I ask how long
till I'm famous, you invite me to scribble
my question on hatchling sea turtles

then release them into the starved Pacific.
When I mutter, "When, when
will you visit?" you have already morphed
into a stab of October light
italicizing a hopscotching six-year-old,
all lope and bounce, singing about tornadoes.

To a Cricket

Darkling fugitive, what do you hope to find
trolling the kitchen at 3:37 a.m.—
a little R & R in the spice rack,
the Northwest Passage of saucer and cup?
I make three empty grabs at your chirps
before landing you in the cage
of my sleepy hand. Should I return you
to my son's tarantula inn, or grant
early Sabbath amnesty? You thrum
like hunger, like old epics buried
in a pawned violin. No, more like a man
opening a door in the dark, taking
harbor in some wilder throat already singing.

To Sunlight Falling in an Old Growth Forest

Who needs a sky bright as forever when I can drown
in refracted green? Thank you, sunlight,
for waking me up to myself. Shadows speak
their gravest truths when you leak in
from above, as if a flock of angels had chewed
summer into lace. And wherever you fall,
a haunting: the good kind that lets me taste
my life without mourning it. I close my eyes.
Each tree a forest of one, each forest a prime
raised to the power of the wandering armadas
in my blood. Teach me to total the world
without counting my fingers, to breathe
in *now* and zero the abacus. I lift a ripe
dandelion to my mouth and scatter the prophets.

To Clouds

Once upon a time, you gathered as firmament.
Once upon a time, you drizzled
on Hannibal and his miracle elephants.
Fell, fall, will fall. Upon Cairo and Calcutta,
upon Tierra del Fuego and the Antipodes,
not to mention upon my hopes
for a decent weekend at the state fair.
The best part of *Hamlet* is watching a tortured
prince use you as a Rorschach test.
Is that a camel floating above our heads . . .
no, a weasel; no, make that a whale,
flukes and all. Now we are smarter.
Now we pin names that stink of Latin
to your lovely hems, try to track
your intentions with oversized balloons.
In the end, I prefer lying on my back
like the next delusional and fishing
your terrifying prairies. Wispy orphans,
you drift in and out of my sadness.
How I would like to brush my teeth
with you, or tie you in a half-Windsor
at my neck. Ah, oracles, ah, handbags of rain,
when I dangle my feet in your Lethe,
swallow me quickly. Gather up
my doubts and misdeeds and sprinkle them
over the next yawning town. But first
show me an oven mitt chasing a crocodile.
But first, the Middle East punch bowl of peace,
with enough tea cups to serve a planet.
But first, the nightgown that nursed me.

To a Braying Donkey

In this thin air, your voice carries a quarter mile,
grating like a train, and I relearn
the ancient lesson—epic sadness travels.
Your braying turns everything tragic.
The face I shave: crossroads of dolor.
The bed I make: labor in lostness.
The scrambled eggs at the end of my fork:
another bite of a century of ills.

I know, I know: everyone needs
to embrace the sad animal of their life.
But must it be first thing each morning?
Can't I look down from my great above
and take pleasure in my neighbor
cutting her father's hair?
For a moment, serenity under the peach tree
among those ripening suns.

Then you kick in, an overdub of snort
and guffaw, and the whole morning turns
jeremiad. Her hands hate their labor.
His dandruffy hair prays not to be chopped.
Even the scissors would prefer
greater purpose, like stabbing a kidnapper
in the neck. Or being left in the cupboard
for a long weekend with the stapler.

Humor? Lamentation? Some mornings
I can't tell the difference. Some mornings
I'm so divided I'd like to join you
in your honking psalms. Roll around
in your sitting room of dust.
Thrust my face into the mossy
bucket and drink deep: where is the *she*
of my asinine dreams, why am I alone in this field?

To My Mother, Chewing

You made the most of every asparagus tip and sliced
peach, every syllable of Waldorf salad,
relaxing as you chewed, fork
hovering, as if obeying some metaphysical *fermata*.
This held true, even if you lacked plate
and utensil and had joined me in the kitchen
to save me from a late dinner alone.
"You're doing it again," I'd say—"trying to help me
eat." And we'd laugh off your vicarious
chewing, some maternal carryover
from baby food days. Still I swallowed
faster than I meant to, lasagna, French bread,
peas, lemon pudding, snatching the world
from your mouth before you had a chance to taste it.

To My Father

Exquisitely hot the August day we buried you,
today eight inches of melting snow.
I park where the gleaming hearse purred.
I've always liked cemeteries, a city shrunk
to a grid of grassy beds, no stop signs,
unpaved lanes dreaming of becoming avenues.

I thought I knew exactly where you lay.
Should have brought a snow shovel and boots.
Listen, why don't you give me a sign?
Perhaps you already have. This zebra piñata
swaying from a tree—your whisper?
This pinwheel stuck in snow—your breath?

Never mind. I'm happy trudging this feeble
circuit, this blank page, letting this scrim of sky
puddle like lost time zones in my shoes.
Is your *there* here, but in another dimension?
Is our *here* a thinner slice of there? Too soon,
I will edge into traffic towards the house

you called home, never mentioning our tryst
of dusk and diminuendo or my failure
to find you. No, I will knock in the dark
and wait for Mom to fumble for the switch,
a ritual you used to live by—wash all prodigals
in a little outside light before inviting them in.

To Breath

What molecules of clean, what scrubbed ozone!
Trout sluice you from fast water,
ants drink you without lungs, while schlubs
like me spend weekends learning
to share you with a dying stranger on a bus.
An intimacy resembling a kiss
but closer to confession. I confess
I've saved no one. I confess wondering,
How many teaspoons of air equal a wind
storm over Laramie, how many of you
are left in me? Don't answer. I'd only spend
my greed trying to extend the contract.
It was different in Eden. When Eve sighed,
her creatures crooned—a caress
of pregnant air sweeter than coupling.
Too bad Adam coughed his way
to an alphabet. Too bad he measured faces
with his sword of words. Couldn't he see
only broken creatures like himself needed names?

To the Lord of Sleepy Places

Taste me Lord the way a generous vintner tastes
a so-so wine, swishing around his mouth

what sat on the shelf too long but had good color.
Spit out my faults, breathe in cool air to set

my smoky bouquet. Never mind Lord
that I might have filled the best crystal goblets

or been lifted to toast an epic journey.
Enough if you taste me in the back of your throat

while humming a blues line in a graveyard
just after dusk to the blurred gossip of fireflies.

To My Radiant Other

You haven't dropped in today, haven't dropped
in for weeks. I feel like a bride
sulking in her veils making excuses
for the one who has jilted her.
Have you abandoned me
for a mender of shoes in Cambodia?

I wander a trail beside a river, trying to make
myself serene, my feet and tumbling
water moving past each other,
like one of those dialogues between sun
and moon. Only I'm less
than the moon of a moon of a moon.

When I was younger you lived inside me,
searching my secret places,
a tireless monk. One moment pressing
my cranium, the next scrunching
in the south pole of my tucked-under toes,
but always sweetly buried,

always specializing in deep ocean sonatas.
Now I'm on my own, a drafty
castle with no fire. I believe in you
most when I am most alone.
Radiant Other, I'm calling
collect, humming you in empty alleys.

Lift my hair, pulse eloquently like a cut
thumb, ooze to the surface
even if there is no surface. Come back,
a vibration of darknesses, a violin
tuning up behind a curtain hung
with crooked stars threatening just now to rise.

V

Something Like Devotion

We're like children floating paper boats down
a canal at midnight. Which if any will reach the pond?

With one hand we test the cold tug of current,
with the other we light the mast, a twisted

paper wick, then aim our tender towards the deep.
Paper racing water, water racing fire, fire

racing paper, three calamities triangulating
our distress, our faces brightest on moonless nights.

Santiago, Pluperfect

Three kids kicking the bejesus out of a taped-up
milk carton and calling it soccer. Pigs
recycling rotten cabbages without being asked.
What we drink in drinks us. In the *feria*,
the melon man with a shriveled arm
pushes a cracked honeydew off his stand.

The splat of green flesh lets him send grabby
urchins to hell while keeping them well fed
for the trip. What burdens we bear
bear us. Shortcuts home add an hour of pastoral
chance to my hurry, past the *Río Maipú,*
past cows re-chewing their boredom under a tree.

A piece of me hangs with the newspaper kite
caught in the power line. Another piece
slumbers in the graveyard in cement beds
stacked six high. What skies we fish fish us.
At the tracks, I copy a pair of wild-haired
sisters and lay three pesos on the rail.

Soon a train to *Valparaíso* will stretch
the face of a dour liberator into something hot
that gleams. I shopped for bread
and accents this morning, and carry home
bread and accents. If angels lodge inside
us, they feed on details, then retreat into hiding.

Like a Wolf

You had to admire the shapeless genius of his outfit—
upside-down garbage bag over purple shorts.
Just a slit for his bald head, holes punched
through for his arms, and a drawstring
he could tighten in case of rain.
I made him my pace car, and tried to stay
no more than five or six strides back.

My purpose: not win or place, just finish.
Like the rest of us, he knew that on race day
triumph must brave leg cramps and wind,
angst and winding climbs, and hope
must first be numbered and pinned to your shorts—
in his case, #88. I loved the symmetry
of those eights. Twin infinity signs standing

upright, one chasing the other the way I was chasing
him. At mile seven, when the sun bled
through red rock hills outside Moab and I tied
my warm-ups at my waist, and real runners flung
theirs into after-race oblivion, I learned
wisdom. Mr. Hefty tore off his garbage bag,
like the Hulk shredding another Armani suit.

And tossed it high. An updraft caught it,
till it floated above what we were, an undulating
river of huff and wheeze pouring out
of the canyon. Floated—an effigy he ran under,
as if he had escaped himself. Old man nipples
peering out at a new world, he tipped
back his head as if drinking the sky and he howled.

This Sadness Machine We Call the Body

Check inside your shoes: not always a scorpion,
sometimes a euro. In most countries,
eating with your hands precedes higher math.
Sky rarely says, You're welcome. Say thank you
anyway. Always wave at the crossing guard.
Secret lovers live in your wrists: do not cut them!

An empty field will forgive you for sudden left turns,
heavy traffic will not. Resist the urge to read
Kafka on your honeymoon. Calm is everywhere
once you squeeze out the meadow larks.
The outside story is called Plot, the inside story
is called Broken Garden Trying to Mend.

A satisfying life will erect a razor-wired fence
separating these two, then spend long weekends
tunneling between. A deaf mother
will weep over her firstborn born deaf,
only rarely out of woe. How to enter a blade
of grass, why the urge to fly but no wings?

Life will grant epiphanic moments to answer
such questions. Now isn't one of them.
What's fun in a Murphy bed rarely lends
itself to franchising. Happiness?
If you're Dutch, plant rare bulbs. If Peruvian,
burn an effigy of yourself New Year's Eve.

Past present future: let tense take turns gargling
your mistakes. Sometimes you hear
Chet Baker only after you turn off the radio.
Never celebrate menopause by passing out
sparklers. Safer to nap in migratory paths
of the dead than jogging paths of the living.

Watching seven deer carom through
an orchard dusted with snow is the quickest
way to book a flight out of your skin.
Never mind the mist. Let the moon sniff you
like a patient lover or pet. Dim the stars,
then sit back to let your new body light the pond.

The Right to Slap Butts, If He Wants

Make that *my butt*, since I've been on
        the receiving end of Knutson's spirited spanks
    all game. Drained a three-pointer—

butt slap one, proof of his affection and esteem.
        At 6' 3", 230, Knut is alpha of the males,
    Mr. Handsome of the recently retired,

Señor Starting Guard at Georgetown then add
        on forty years. If he had the right to lay on
    hands back then, he has it in spades

these days after going up for a bound last
        spring and coming down clutching his heart.
    Some minutes back when I finessed

a finger-roll lay-in, Knutson dished out butt swat two—
        to my left cheek, so at least the sting of praise
    was balanced. He nodded at me, frog-eyed

through his goggles, and I recalled the EMTs
        fussing over him, a pair of mechanics bringing back
    a stalled compressor from the dead.

Mr. Delay of Game, Mr. Three-Second
        Violation that lasted till they gurneyed him away.
    These days he's in the thick of it again,

talking trash under his breath, wrestling loose balls
        like a rookie, Knutson with a Frankenstein scar
    down his sternum, where they ratcheted

open his ribs to re-plumb his heart.
          Just now attempting a fadeaway, I got stuffed
     so clean and mean by a shaved-head punk,

that Knutson delivered butt slap three—
          but this one rueful, less sting, a consolation slap.
     Call me Knut, it says—a buck who's been around

the block. Never mind the geezer the mirror
          gives back, keep waking up, hurt your enemies
     but only till you halfway love them, we're half dead,

every one of us, happy dribbling corpses.
          Can't you, this defeat, my friend, never mind,
     already taste it, Lord Lord give us more.

Late Morning Salvage

And now a calico stray ankles along
begging me to pick her up and breathe

her sacred groves, and now a ruby throat
mistakes my striped shirt for Eden

and tries to drink my bum shoulder—
ah, the pleasures of waiting like a peasant

for the next life. I can almost hear
the search party above dragging the lake,

all curses and oars and grappling hooks,
placing bets on how quickly I'll be found.

Solving for Clean

I drop off my broken shoes to a Brazilian cobbler
in the strip mall, my shirts to a laundress
from Laos who has set up shop
where 7-Eleven used to be. I need someone
I can trust to turn my feet straight again,
someone to treat me like a proper parable of grit
and solve for *Clean*. Sure, if a tumor bloomed,

sui generis behind my eye, I might want
my English straight. But for everyday errands
of the body—soiled shirts, shoes worn down
as if a penguin had waddled from Tierra del Fuego—
I'll take grunts and whistles every time.
I leave my words at the door, helpless
crutches, and let my animal talk to their animal.

Nods, followed by more vigorous nods.
"Tuesday okay four," he says.
"Friday good yes," she says, and the spinning
globe resets its clock to their pidgin.
How I'd like to find some Calcutta uncle
to plumb the dark harbors of this frame,
some Sudanese widow to thaw my arctic winters.

Hand signals and truthful exhalations
of the flesh. Comforting the way Mr. Brazil
hops my shoes through air,
like twin bunnies sprung from a trap,
the way this laundress shakes her head
at my shirts, ghosts that need a bath,
sooty ghosts only she knows how to brighten.

Three Things That Fit in Your Pocket

Each morning finds her parked outside
El Metro on a patch of dirt,
pregnant, eager to sell her wares
spread across a beach towel
featuring pink sea horses
playing sax. Anciently, she might
have suckled seven children and a wolf cub.

Or mourned her husband at war by weaving
a tapestry out of bird song
and the babble of leaves.
Back then, if you hoped to keep
your girl parts to yourself, you learned
to shun every shower of gold,
every lusty swan floating like an invitation.

Back then, if pursuit got dicey you turned
into a babbling brook.
Today, brooks flow few and far between.
Today peasant girls sell. I hand her
what I have, pesos. She hands me
what I didn't know I needed. Gum.
Batteries. A charm dipped in pigeon blood.

I am what I am: a stranger to Santiago,
but for the rest of the day,
a blessed stranger—my mouth minty,
my dead radio singing arias, my shirt collar
protecting me from the Evil Eye.
When she smiles I hypothesize two men:
one who got her pregnant, one who bruised

her left cheek. I hope they do not both
answer to husband. I hope
the child she carries answers to desire,
not coercion. She nods.
Until some new myth converts
her seahorse towel and economy
of kneeling into dignity, I nod back.

If business fails to pick up, let her take
her merchandise downtown,
where buses run free—
as long as you're a peasant selling
or singing, as long as you travel
just two stops at a time,
as long as you get off before you arrive.

Acknowledgments

I gratefully acknowledge the editors of the following journals and anthologies in which these poems, sometimes under different titles, previously appeared:

Agni:	"The Right to Slap Butts, If He Wants"
Alaska Quarterly Review:	"Make of Me"
Best American Poetry 2009:	"Why Do You Keep Putting Animals in Your Poems?" (reprint)
Brevity:	"Tired"
Chariton Review:	"To My Mother, Chewing"
Connotation Press:	"The Most Spider Part of Me"
Crab Orchard Review:	"Americana"
Crazyhorse:	"To Jouissance"
Field:	"After De Chirico"
	"Rough Translation"
	"To a Cricket"
Fire in the Pasture:	"Backyard Georgics" (reprint)
	"To the Ode" (reprint)
	"Why Do You Keep Putting Animals in Your Poems?" (reprint)
Folio:	"To Duende"
Georgia Review:	"To Alchemy"
Great River Review:	"Late Morning Salvage"
Green Mountains Review:	"A Bright Darkness Sometimes Mistaken for Fishing"
Image:	"When the Lord Returns in All His Creaturely Perfection"
	"Tabernacle"
Indiana Review:	"Why Do You Keep Putting Animals in Your Poems?"
Likewise Folio:	"To Breath"
New Ohio Review:	"Between the Heaves of Storm"
	"What Bliss When Exuberance Overruns its Banks"
Nimrod:	"Like a Wolf"
Orion:	"Chancellor of Shadows"
Ploughshares:	"To a Braying Donkey"
Poets of the American West:	"Americana" (reprint)
	"Like a Wolf" (reprint)
	"Why Do You Keep Putting Animals in Your Poems?" (reprint)

Poetry:	"Backyard Georgics"
POW: the Provo Orem Word:	"A Magpie's Hop" (broadside reprint)
	"Make of Me" (reprint)
	"To My Mother, Chewing" (reprint)
	"To the Ode" (reprint)
Prairie Schooner:	"Adding a Certain Ghost-like Hum to Your Inner Life"
	"Elegy, with City Bus and Blue-haired Girl"
	"Owning the Snake"
	"To Clouds"
	"To My Father"
	"To the Ode"
Quarterly West:	"Garden of Earthly Delights"
Raritan:	"Nothing Happy"
	"Something Like Devotion"
	"Three Things that Fit in Your Pocket"
	"To My Radiant Other"
River Styx:	"Man in a Suit, Twelve Crickets in His Pocket"
Slate:	"Santiago, Pluperfect"
Southern Review:	"Solving for Clean"
	"This Sadness Machine We Call the Body"
	"To My Insomnia"
	"To My Muse"
	"To the Lord of Sleepy Places"
Tampa Review:	"A Magpie's Hop"
	"To Sunlight Falling in an Old Growth Forest"

ART WORKS.
arts.gov

I am indebted to the National Endowment for the Arts, the Anderson Center, and the Virginia Center for the Creative Arts for fellowships that made the writing of this collection possible. Thanks as well to the College of Humanities at Brigham Young University for its crucial support.

Ongoing gratitude to Shannon Castleton, Scott Hatch, Michael Hicks, Susan Howe, David Nielsen, and Natasha Sajé, for their sympathetic scalpels; to Richard Mathews, for his advocacy and bonhomie; and to Jacqui, my Beatrice and co-conspirator, for seeing me through.

About the Author and the Artist

Lance Larsen, poet laureate of Utah, is the author of three previous collections: *Erasable Walls* (1998); *In All Their Animal Brilliance* (2005), which won the Tampa Review Prize; and *Backyard Alchemy* (2009). His poems have appeared in such venues as *Slate, Poetry, Raritan, Southern Review, River Styx, Orion, Raritan, Georgia Review, Ploughshares, Verse Daily*, and *Best American Poetry 2009*. He holds a PhD from the University of Houston and teaches at Brigham Young University, where he serves as MFA coordinator. He has received a number of awards, including a Pushcart Prize and a 2007 fellowship from the National Endowment for the Arts. He is married to painter and mixed-media artist Jacqui Larsen, with whom he has directed study abroad programs in London and Madrid.

Jacqui Larsen has shown her work in New York, Illinois, Texas, Utah, California, and at the Millennium Arts Center in Washington, D.C. The recipient of numerous grants, awards, and fellowships, she uses found text, patterns, and images in both her collages and paintings. Her work can be seen online at www.jacquilarsen.com.

About the Book

Genius Loci is set in Perpetua types, created by Eric Gill in the late 1920s and first used for a limited edition of *The Passion of Perpetua and Felicity*, the work from which the type received its name. The book of *Genius Loci* was designed and typeset by Richard Mathews at the University of Tampa Press. It has been printed with wind energy on acid-free recycled text paper in support of the Green Press Initiative.

POETRY FROM THE UNIVERSITY OF TAMPA PRESS

John Blair, *The Occasions of Paradise**

Jenny Browne, *At Once*

Jenny Browne, *The Second Reason*

Christopher Buckley, *Rolling the Bones**

Christopher Buckley, *White Shirt*

Richard Chess, *Chair in the Desert*

Richard Chess, *Tekiah*

Richard Chess, *Third Temple*

Kevin Jeffery Clarke, *The Movie of Us*

Jane Ellen Glasser, *Light Persists**

Benjamin S. Grossberg, *Sweet Core Orchard**

Dennis Hinrichsen, *Rip-tooth**

Kathleen Jesme, *Fire Eater*

Steve Kowit, *The First Noble Truth**

Lance Larsen, *Backyard Alchemy*

Lance Larsen, *Genius Loci*

Lance Larsen, *In All Their Animal Brilliance**

Julia B. Levine, *Ask**

Julia B. Levine, *Ditch-tender*

Sarah Maclay, *Whore**

Sarah Maclay, *The White Bride*

Sarah Maclay, *Music for the Black Room*

Peter Meinke, *Lines from Neuchâtel*

John Willis Menard, *Lays in Summer Lands*

Kent Shaw, *Calenture**

Barry Silesky, *This Disease*

Jordan Smith, *For Appearances**

Jordan Smith, *The Names of Things Are Leaving*

Jordan Smith, *The Light in the Film*

Lisa M. Steinman, *Carslaw's Sequences*

Marjorie Stelmach, *Bent upon Light*

Marjorie Stelmach, *A History of Disappearance*

Ira Sukrungruang, *In Thailand It Is Night* ◊

Richard Terrill, *Coming Late to Rachmaninoff*

Richard Terrill, *Almost Dark*

Matt Yurdana, *Public Gestures*

* Denotes winner of the Tampa Review Prize for Poetry
◊ Denotes winnter of the Anita Claire Scharf Prize